The workhouse treat: a watercolour by John Henry Buckingham of a summer treat for the inmates of St Albans workhouse, Hertfordshire, probably in the 1850s. Both male and female paupers wear uniform clothing, the women – as befitted a centre of the straw-hat industry – sporting jaunty straw bonnets. One of the treats in store is a pipe of tobacco, for a hamper with clay churchwarden pipes is to be seen in the bottom left-hand corner.

THE VICTORIAN WORKHOUSE

Trevor May

Shire Publications Ltd

CONTENTS

Published in 2005 by Shire Publications Ltd, Cromwell House, Church Street, Princes Risborough, Buckinghamshire HP27 9AA, UK.
Website: www.shirebooks.co.uk
Copyright © 1997 by Trevor May. First published 1997; reprinted 1999, 2000, 2002, 2003 and 2005.
Shire Album 334. ISBN 0 7478 0355 2.
Trevor May is hereby identified as the author of this work in accordance with Section 77 of the Copyright, Designs and Patents Act 1988.

Printed in Great Britain by CIT Printing Services Ltd, Press Buildings, Merlins Bridge, Haverfordwest, Pembrokeshire SA61 1XF.

British Library Cataloguing in Publication Data: May, Trevor. The Victorian Workhouse. – (Shire album; 334) Almshouses – Great Britain – History – 19th century 2. Almshouses – Great Britain – Design and construction I. Title 362.5'8'5'0941'09034 ISBN 0 7478 0355 2

ACKNOWLEDGEMENTS

For help in the preparation of this book I wish to thank Anthony Chadwick of the Ripon Workhouse Museum, and my wife, Jennifer, who accepted many detours in order to visit workhouses.

Illustrations are acknowledged as follows: Andover Museum (Hampshire County Council Museums Service), page 25 (top); British Newspaper Library, pages 4 (top), 24 (left); reproduced by kind permission of Doncaster Libraries, page 20 (bottom); Hampshire Record Office, page 18 (bottom); London Borough of Harrow Education Services, page 5 (top right); Newcastle Libraries and Information Services, page 8; Pontefract Museum, page 25 (bottom); Norfolk Museum of Rural Life, pages 21 (top right and centre right), 22 (top right); St Albans Museum, page 1; Somerset County Museums Service, page 21 (top left); Charles and Harold Walker and the Otley Museum, page 13 (centre and bottom). Other illustrations are taken from contemporary publications, the source being identified in the caption, or are photographs by the author.

Cover: *Detail from 'Eventide' by Sir Hubert von Herkomer, 1878. Almost the only known painting of a workhouse interior, it shows old women in the Westminster workhouse. Reproduced by permission of the Board of Trustees of the National Museums and Galleries on Merseyside (Walker Art Gallery, Liverpool).*

Left: *Our view of workhouse architecture may be one of drab uniformity, but architects often took pride in introducing some individual element, such as the pair of 'pepper pot' gatehouses designed by George Wilkinson at Thame in Oxfordshire.*

The garret of a military tailor and his family in Bethnal Green, London (an engraving from the Illustrated London News, 24th October 1863). Many economists and commentators justified poverty on the grounds that it alone motivated the masses to work. It was only when people sank so deep into poverty that they were unable to support themselves that the Poor Law stepped in.

THE BASIS OF THE VICTORIAN POOR LAW

The Victorians loved a biblical text but they did not always seem too concerned about using it in context. 'If any would not work, neither should he eat,' wrote St Paul, while Jesus said: 'For ye have the poor always with you.' Christ's words seemed demonstrably true in the nineteenth century, and many did not regret the fact, for poverty was seen to have positive benefits, if not to the poor themselves, then to society as a whole. The pamphleteer and police reformer Patrick Colquhoun wrote in 1806: 'Poverty is...a most necessary and indispensable ingredient in society... It is the lot of man – it is the source of wealth, since without poverty there would be no labour, and without labour there could be no riches, no refinement, no comfort, and no benefit to those who may be possessed of wealth. Indigence therefore, and not poverty, is the evil. It is that condition in society which implies want, misery, and distress. It is the state of anyone who is destitute of the means of subsistence, and is unable to labour to procure it

to the extent nature requires.'

It was only the indigent (the paupers) who needed the services of the Poor Law. The merely poor could fend for themselves, with the aid of that Christian charity which they made possible in others. Acts of charity might be individual; they might spring from a church or chapel congregation; or they might be the product of a vast bureaucracy. In the early 1860s it was calculated that philanthropic activity in London alone amounted to between £5.5 and £7 million annually, a figure not far short of the total expenditure on the Poor Law throughout the whole of England and Wales.

When poor relief was overhauled between 1832 and 1834, the reformers saw it as their task to return to the spirit of the Elizabethan Poor Law and to set the poor to work. An Act of 1601 had laid down that each parish was to be responsible for the maintenance of its own paupers, the responsibility falling on annually appointed overseers who would have the

Left: *A page of advertisements from the Poor-Law Officers' Journal, 2nd March 1900. Garrould's advertisement reflects the trend whereby workhouses increasingly became refuges for the elderly and the sick, with the result that many ended up either as old people's homes or as hospitals. On the other hand, Brundrit & Company's offer of Penmaenmawr granite for stone breaking demonstrates that the idea of the 'workhouse test' had not disappeared in the case of the vagrant poor.*

Opposite page, top left: *The workhouse was not an appropriate remedy for short periods of industrial distress. At such times out-relief was resorted to, while charitable responses such as the soup kitchen were common. That shown here was operated by Quakers in Manchester in 1852. (Engraving from the Illustrated London News, 22nd November 1852.)*

Opposite page, top right: *Before 1834, parishes might 'privatise' the care of the poor by inviting tenders to run the workhouse. The contractor who was prepared to undertake the work for the lowest figure generally got the job; but he always felt pressure to stint on his provision for the poor, in order to maximise his profit. 'Farming the poor' was not an inapt description of these arrangements. 'Expenses of removals' relates to the 'settlement laws' which empowered the authorities to remove a pauper back to the parish where he or she was 'settled', and which therefore had liability for poor relief. Settlement could be obtained in a variety of ways, including birth, marriage and possession of a contract of employment lasting a year and a day.*

Charities co-existed with the Poor Law in the nineteenth century. Old-established almshouses continued to be used, and many new ones were constructed. Hosyer's Almshouses, in Ludlow, Shropshire, were rebuilt in 1758 and remain in use to this day. The provision of charitable aid was often greater in ancient towns like Ludlow (with a population of around five thousand in 1851) than it was in the new industrial towns, where the poor existed in greater numbers.

Below: *Parish workhouses occasionally displayed considerable style, as in the case of that at Harrogate, North Yorkshire (now Starbeck Hall). Built in 1810-11, it was run by the parish overseers until 1854, when the Poor Law Board finally secured the establishment of the Harrogate and Knaresborough Union. Four years later it was superseded by a new union workhouse built in Knaresborough.*

ove: *Parish workhouses before 1834 usually lacked the bidding aspects of their New Poor Law successors. They re often constructed on a domestic scale, as in the case of Aldenham, Hertfordshire, workhouse shown here. When d in 1838, it was described by the auctioneers as a 'SUB-NTIAL BRICK Built and TILED BUILDING...Divided into Numer-s Spacious and Lofty Apartments...BEAUTIFULLY SITUATED NEAR CHURCH'. The building was subsequently converted into a v of cottages.*

power to levy a poor rate. The elderly and the sick were to be maintained, and work was to be provided for the able-bodied, in workhouses set up for that purpose.

By the eighteenth century a number of expedients other than the workhouse had crept into the system, and there was considerable regional variation in the administration of poor relief. These measures included the roundsman system, where unemployed labourers were sent round the parish from one farm to another until someone was willing to take them on for a wage subsidised by the parish; and the imposition of a labour rate, which compelled each ratepayer to employ a certain number of labourers according to his

poor-rate assessment, or to pay the parish a sum equal to their wages if he had no work. Most common, however, was the allowance system (sometimes referred to as the Speenhamland system) whereby wages were subsidised on a scale which was determined both by the price of bread and the number of persons in the labourer's family.

In the decades after the end of the Napoleonic wars there was a marked increase in the cost of poor relief, from around £2 million in 1784 to roughly £7 million in 1832. Something, it was felt, had to be done. That something was to set up a commission of inquiry, which sat from 1832 to 1834. In what was a pioneering piece of government fact-gathering, questionnaires were sent to each of the fifteen thousand parishes of England and Wales. Only about 10 per cent of the parishes bothered to reply, and so twenty-six Assistant Commissioners were sent out to

Right: *In the early years of the New Poor Law, pauperism was predominantly a rural problem. This cartoon by John Leech appeared in Punch in 1843. Agricultural societies frequently awarded prizes not only for livestock but also to labourers, who were rewarded for the constancy of their service or for their ability to support their families off the poor rate. In one of the accompanying verses, the labourer is given to bewail the sense of priorities which awards lower prizes for men than for animals:*
> *'My children and wife I have kept all my life*
> *From off the parish clear:*
> *But merit like mine, to the worth of a swine,*
> *People think small beer.'*

THE RIVALS.

PRIZE PEASANT. PRIZE PIG.

Plate V. —— COLD, MISERY, AND WANT, DESTROY THEIR YOUNGEST CHILD; THEY CONSOLE THEMSELVES WITH THE BOTTLE.

Left: *Throughout the nineteenth century the prevailing view amongst the middle and upper classes was that pauperism resulted from individual failing. This might express itself through improvidence, reckless child-bearing or intemperance. In 1847 George Cruikshank issued a series of etchings entitled 'The Bottle', charting the decline of a happy and thriving family as a result of drink. The father of the family, crazed with alcohol, kills his wife and ends up in an asylum. His children take to the streets to keep themselves from the workhouse. This particular etching is the fifth of the series of eight.*

Right: *Charles Dickens started his novel 'Oliver Twist' in 1837, three years after the passage of the Poor Law Amendment Act. Internal evidence would indicate that Oliver was born in a workhouse under the Old Poor Law, but his presumption in 'asking for more' illustrated a harshness of regime which applied equally to the new workhouses.*

PUNCH'S PENCILLINGS. — Nº LXII.

George Cruikshank

THE "MILK" OF POOR-LAW "KINDNESS."

Left: *Like The Times, Punch could be scathing in its attacks on the New Poor Law. This cartoon appeared in 1843 and was prompted by a claim made by a ratepayer of Bethnal Green that 'An infant, only five weeks old, was separated from the mother, being occasionally brought to her for the breast'. Many such stories were mythical, but the authorities did little to rebut them for they helped to instil a fear of the new workhouses.*

The New Starvation Law examined,

And some Description of the Food, Dress, Labour, and Regulations, imposed upon the poor and unfortunate Sufferers in the New British Bastiles.

Come you men and women unto me attend,
And listen and see what for you I have penn'd;
And if you do buy it, and carefully read,
'T will make your hearts within you to bleed.

The lions at London, with their cruel paw,
You know they have pass'd a Starvation Law;
These tigers and wolves should be chained in a den,
Without power to worry poor women and men.

Like the fox in the farm-yard they slily do creep;
These hard-hearted wretches, O, how dare they sleep,
To think they should pass such a law in our day,
To hate and to stop the poor widow's pay.

And if they don't like their pay to be stopp'd,
'Gainst their own will into th' Bastile they're popp'd;
Their homes must break up, and never return,
But leave their relations and children to mourn.

The three pension'd paupers in grandeur do live,
Pon riches that they from the taxes receive;
Which poor people pay from their scanty week's wage,
Though pinch'd, and confin'd like a bird in a cage.

But if they'd to work before they were fed,
They'd not go a tolling the poor children's bread,
Which fathers do earn very hard every day,
While they in carriages are dashing away.

There's many poor children go ragged and torn,
While they and their horses are pamper'd with corn;
Now is not this world quite unequally dealt?
The Starvation Law by some few is felt.

When a man and his wife for sixty long years
Have toiled together through troubles and fears,
And brought up a family with prudence and care,
To be sent to the Bastile it's very unfair.

And in the Bastile each woman and man
Is parted asunder,—is this a good plan?
A word of sweet comfort they cannot express,
For unto each other they ne'er have access.

Of their uniform, too, you something shall hear,—
In strong Fearnaught jackets the men do appear;
In coarse Grogram gowns the women do shine,
And a ninepenny cap,—now won't they be fine?

On fifteenpence halfpenny they keep them a week;
I'nd Commissioners this we should have them to seek,
They'd not come to Yorkshire to visit us here,
And of such vile vermin we soon should be clear.

To give them hard labour, it is understood,
In handmills the grain they must grind for their food,
Like men in a prison they work them in gangs,
With turning and twisting it fills them with pangs.

I'll give you an insight of their regulations,
Which they put in force in these situations,
They've no school, chapel, and prison all under a roof,
And the governor's house stands a little aloof.

The master instructs them the law to obey,
The governor minds it's all work and no play,
And as for religion the parson doth teach
That he knows the gospel,—no other must preach.

Ye hard-working men, wherever you be,
I'd have you watch closely these men, d'ye see;
I think they're contriving, the country all o'er,
To see what's the worst they can do to the poor.

But if that their incomes you wish for to touch,
They'll vapour, and grumble, and talk very much,
The Corn Laws uphold, the poor will oppress,
And send them to th' Bastile in th' day of distress.

R. H.

Opposition to the New Poor Law was strong in the north of England and discontent was often expressed in the form of the cheaply printed broadsheet. This example was produced by Reuben Holder of Bradford. Resistance in that city was violent but short, although a new workhouse was not built until 1852. The Todmorden union, which served parishes in Lancashire as well as Yorkshire, held out even longer. Not until 1877 was its new workhouse constructed, making it the last in England. This ballad rails at many things, including the separation of families. In the ninth verse it puts the question: 'And in the Bastile each woman and man/ Is parted asunder, – is this a good plan?'

bring back the information and they visited about a fifth of the Poor Law authorities. Their evidence, when finally published, filled thirteen volumes, containing a total of nearly eight thousand pages. It might be thought that sifting through this mountain of data would have taken the nine Commissioners a considerable period of time, but not so. They were under great pressure from the government to act with speed, and this they did. Indeed, the report was written and despatched to the printers even before all the evidence was in. This is no great surprise. They knew what they expected to find – and they found it. They also knew what they would recommend.

The two leading lights of the Commission, who between them wrote most of the report, were Edwin Chadwick and Nassau Senior. Both were followers of the philosopher Jeremy Bentham (1748-1832), who believed that all human action was motivated by the seeking of pleasure and the avoidance of pain. This principle was to be applied to poor relief. The writer Thomas Carlyle cynically observed: 'If paupers are made miserable, paupers will needs decline in multitude. It is a secret known to all rat-catchers.' The principles of the report were incorporated in the Poor Law Amendment Act of 1834. A central body of three Poor Law Commissioners was to be set up in London and, acting through Assistant Commissioners, they were to supervise the combination of parishes into Poor Law unions. This had previously been permitted by private Act of Parliament, and Gilbert's Act of 1782 had simplified the procedure. It was now to be made compulsory, and over thirteen thousand parishes would be incorporated into 573 unions by 1838. Not until 1868 was the whole country covered, and even then there remained areas covered by private Act which remained exempt.

All able-bodied persons who sought poor relief were to be given it – but only within a workhouse, the conditions in which were to be made 'less eligible' (i.e. more miserable) than those of the poorest independent labourer. According to Benthamite principles, the applicant would have passed 'the workhouse test'. He or she would have weighed the 'pleasures' of staying outside the workhouse with the 'pain' of entering it, and only the truly destitute would accept relief. Such was the theory. In practice things did not work out quite so simply.

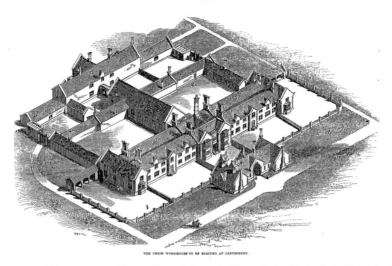

THE UNION WORKHOUSE TO BE ERECTED AT CANTERBURY.

Bird's-eye view of Canterbury workhouse, Kent, designed by Henry Walter Parker in 1846. While the able-bodied were to be confined behind high walls, children and the elderly were merely kept in by an open fence. It was observed that at Aylesbury workhouse, Buckinghamshire, erected to the same design, 'the aged inmates have converted their airing-yard into a pleasant garden, where they may be seen tending shrubs and flowers with as much care as they would bestow on the culture of similar plants in their cottage gardens'. (Engraving from the Illustrated London News, 7th November 1846.)

THE DESIGN AND CONSTRUCTION OF WORKHOUSES

The Act of 1834 had an immediate impact on the landscape, as union workhouses were erected at a distance of roughly 20 miles (32 km) from each other. In the following five years some 350 were constructed, most of them being in the more agricultural and more pauperised south of England. By 1883 a total of 554 new workhouses had been built.

In their first Annual Report, published in 1835, the Poor Law Commissioners included an appendix containing a number of model plans for workhouses. They accepted that 'deviations from them might be necessary to meet local circumstances', but they possessed the safeguard that all plans submitted by local boards of guardians had to be approved by them. The first of the designs was for a rural workhouse for five hundred paupers and was drawn by Francis Bond Head, an Assistant Commissioner in Kent, where the plans were mainly adopted. Head took the view that 'the height of the rooms, the thickness of the walls, &c., &c., should not exceed the dimensions of the cottage of the labourer; well-built, substantial rooms being a luxury as attractive to the pauper as food and raiment'. In consequence, he allowed only 6 feet (1.83 metres) headroom in the upper floors of his workhouse.

Far more influential were the designs of Sampson Kempthorne (1809-73). Critics argued, though without being able to substantiate their claim, that Kempthorne, who had not long been in practice, lifted his ideas directly from contemporary American prison design, and from the 'Panopticon' of Jeremy Bentham. In the 1790s Bentham had developed his idea, adaptable to many uses, of a circular building in which observation of all parts was possible from a central core, and the principle had become widely known. None of Kempthorne's designs was circular, however, and, although a central block was a feature, it allowed observation of the yards

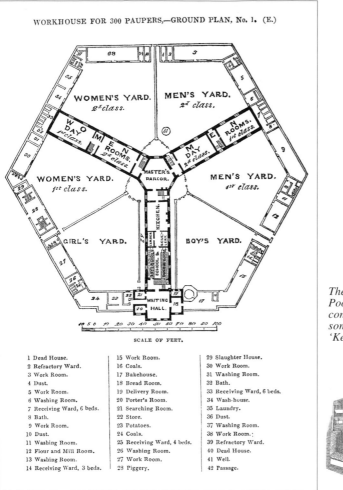

SCALE OF FEET.

The first Annual Report of the Poor Law Commissioners in 1835 contained this hexagonal plan, sometimes referred to as the 'Kempthorne star'.

PERSPECTIVE VIEW OF A WORKHOUSE FOR 300 PAUPERS. (E.)

1 Dead House.	15 Work Room.	29 Slaughter House.
2 Refractory Ward.	16 Coals.	30 Work Room.
3 Work Room.	17 Bakehouse.	31 Washing Room.
4 Dust.	18 Bread Room.	32 Bath.
5 Work Room.	19 Delivery Room.	33 Receiving Ward, 6 beds.
6 Washing Room.	20 Porter's Room.	34 Wash-house.
7 Receiving Ward, 6 beds.	21 Searching Room.	35 Laundry.
8 Bath.	22 Store.	36 Dust.
9 Work Room.	23 Potatoes.	37 Washing Room.
10 Dust.	24 Coals.	38 Work Room.;
11 Washing Room.	25 Receiving Ward, 4 beds.	39 Refractory Ward.
12 Flour and Mill Room.	26 Washing Room.	40 Dead House.
13 Washing Room.	27 Work Room.	41 Well.
14 Receiving Ward, 3 beds.	28 Piggery.	42 Passage.

only, and not of the internal arrangement of the buildings.

Kempthorne, who also drew up plans for elementary schools for the Committee of the Council on Education, designed a number of workhouses before he emigrated to New Zealand in 1841-2. These included Abingdon, the first workhouse to accommodate five hundred paupers to be completed after the Act, which cost £9000.

Both the cruciform plan and the 'Y' plan (sometimes known as the hexagonal plan because of the curtain walls, and sometimes as the 'Kempthorne star') were well adapted, in theory if not in practice, to the new Poor Law principles of the classification and separation of paupers. The Commissioners of 1832-4 had principally been concerned to get rid of out-relief and had therefore spent less of their time critically examining the existing workhouses. They had, however, condemned the 'general mixed workhouse', where the able-bodied and the elderly, the sick and the young, the workless and

10

One of the porters' lodges (left) of Aylesbury workhouse, Buckinghamshire, designed by Assistant Poor Law Commissioner Henry Walter Parker. The workhouse was opened in 1844, and it was reported that 'from the windows...there is a delightful view of the Chiltern Hills'. But within a year the new County Gaol had been erected on the opposite side of road, completely blocking the view (right). The juxtaposition of workhouse and prison tells us much about Victorian attitudes to the lower classes.

the work-shy had spent their time in each other's company. The Commissioners therefore laid it down as a principle that those who sought relief in the workhouse should be divided into groups. It was a flawed principle from the start, largely because the classification proved inadequate. Men were to be separated from women (thus breaking up families), and both groups were to be divided into the able-bodied, the aged and children. However, no proper provision was made for the sick and the mentally ill, and vagrants were totally ignored. The original idea that the different groups should be housed in separate workhouses (adapting the existing parochial buildings) was speedily dropped, partly on the grounds of cost; but it also proved unworkable in that families had to be admitted and discharged together, giving rise to considerable problems when individual members were scattered over a wide area. Almost from the start, therefore, the single union work-

house became the norm; and almost from the start it began to slip back towards the mixed workhouse. On the other hand, the union workhouse exerted a psychological force far greater than that of the parish workhouses, which had often been built on a domestic scale. Opponents of the new workhouses referred to them as 'bastilles' (often spelled 'bastiles', and apparently pronounced with a long 'i'), and it suited the Commissioners' plans of deterrence that they should do so.

The Institute of British Architects had been incorporated in 1834 (it acquired the title 'Royal' four years later), and workhouse building provided opportunities for many established and aspiring members of the architectural profession. Of none was this more true than George Gilbert Scott (1811-78), who in the course of a long career was responsible for over one thousand new buildings or restoration projects, of which workhouses were the most lowly and most forgotten. Scott

When George Gilbert Scott designed Amersham workhouse, Buckinghamshire, in 1838 his Elizabethan design incorporated much flint, a prominent local building material. The 'AV' picked out in brickwork refers to the Amersham Union. Like the Romans, it seems, the bricklayers did not recognise the letter U.

Tavistock workhouse in Devon (1837) was one of a number designed by the partnership of George Gilbert Scott and William Bonython Moffatt. The plan resembles Kempthorne's cruciform workhouse, but with the forward-facing arm truncated. In its place is a courtyard, to which access is gained through an imposing central archway. This former workhouse is now used as flats, and although the painting of the exterior walls gives the buildings a less forbidding appearance than they would have had, the sense of isolation that typified many workhouses is still to be felt.

worked as an assistant to Kempthorne and occupied neighbouring chambers in Regent Street, London. Later he embarked on his own, shortly afterwards entering into a partnership with William Bonython Moffatt. For a decade Scott and Moffatt worked feverishly on workhouse designs, eventually producing over fifty. With so many workhouses being erected at around the same time, Scott and Moffatt put enormous energy into securing commissions. 'For weeks', Scott later wrote, 'I almost lived on horseback, canvassing newly formed unions.' Such was the pace that on one occasion Scott telegraphed his office from a provincial railway station with the desperate query: 'Why am I here?' Every week the two young architects visited a London coffee-house to scour the country papers in order to pick up details of tenders being invited or competitions held. Soon workhouses designed by Scott and Moffatt, either individually or in partnership, were to be found from Lincolnshire to Cornwall.

Boards of guardians faced a number of constraints when erecting workhouses. That essential but noxious public services should be located 'not in my back yard' was a view common to nineteenth- as well as twentieth-century taxpayers. Guardians were therefore impelled to choose a site that was reasonably central to the union, so that paupers might more easily walk to the workhouse, while at the same time attempting to allow them no nearer than the very periphery of towns. The minutes of the guardians of Hitchin in Hertfordshire exemplify the concern. Their new workhouse, designed by the local architect Thomas Smith of Hertford, was opened at Chalkdells, away from the town, in December 1836. Four months later the master was directed to permit the aged and infirm poor in the workhouse to have the privilege, if well-behaved, of walking in the workhouse grounds. Since the nearest building to the new workhouse was half a mile (800 metres) away, it was argued that the promenading would in no

Right: *The Poor Law Board Act of 1847 contained a clause requiring boards of guardians to provide any married couple over sixty with a separate bedroom in the workhouse, if requested. Fifty years later, in the whole of England and Wales, there were still only two hundred married couples who enjoyed their own room. (Illustration from 'Living London', 1901.)*

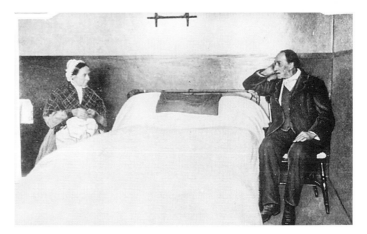

Below and left: : *Otley workhouse, West Yorkshire, in the early twentieth century. Although this picture appears to be of a day-room for aged men, a youth is to be seen behind the chair. The floorboards are bare and the room has an austere appearance, but there is a good fire and there is gaslight. Moreover, the chairs have backs. In the early years of the New Poor Law, the elderly in many workhouses were required to sit on backless benches, for the sake of 'less eligibility'. The second picture, originally captioned 'Rest room for permanent women inmates' gives a cosier impression, with prints on the wall and a variety of knick-knacks on the mantlepiece.*

way 'discommode or prove offensive to the citizens'.

Boards of guardians were also constrained by cost, and here civic pride (especially in the towns) vied with the need for economy. The result is that many workhouses have an elegant public face, disguising the meaner accommodation within. A second wave of workhouse building took place in the 1860s and 1870s, much of it located in the north of England, where civic rivalry was intense. George Goschen, President of the Poor Law Board between 1868 and 1871,

Many workhouses in the north of England were built twenty or thirty years after the majority in the agricultural south. The workhouse at Ripon in North Yorkshire proudly announces the date of its establishment in 1854. The plans were drawn up by Perkins and Backhouse, the Leeds-based firm of architects who seven years previously had designed Armley Gaol in what Nikolaus Pevsner describes as 'the accepted dungeon style'. The workhouse at Ripon is altogether more gentle, both in scale and aspect, and now houses a museum of Yorkshire workhouse history.

railed against extravagant architectural detail, including 'granite columns, terra-cotta moulding, encaustic tile pavements, Portland stone decorations, and so on'. Whatever the location or the scale of the workhouse, and at whatever time it was erected, it was the least used room that was generally the most ostentatious – the boardroom, where the guardians held their mandatory fortnightly meetings. Styles varied, but in 1865 the *Social Science Review* pictured the typical boardroom as 'a mixture of an Old Bailey court, a small chapel, and a third class railway waiting room'.

When visiting a former workhouse, it can be very difficult to work out the function of particular buildings or rooms, and this is so even if the visitor has a copy of the original plan. Not only have buildings been remodelled to fit their post-workhouse functions, but even in their heyday workhouses underwent frequent changes as they

became subject to different pressures. The historian Peter Wood has given the example of Sunderland workhouse, which was opened in 1838 but was regarded as inadequate within a year. A proposal to build a new three-storey wing was shelved in favour of a plan to make fuller use of the attics and basement. The former were converted to dormitories and the latter to day-rooms, increasing the capacity of the workhouse by 50 per cent. Under continuing pressure, a mangle room became a day-room, while former day-rooms were converted into sick wards. The need for additional hospital accommodation was accepted in 1846, but that had to await the opening of a new workhouse in 1855. Within five years the process had begun again, in order to meet fresh demands for the accommodation of children and the sick. Students of workhouses will find similar changes wherever they look.

STAFFING THE WORKHOUSE

The responsibility for building the new workhouses, and for staffing and administering them, fell on locally elected boards of guardians. They were often resentful of central direction from London and did their best to circumvent it when it proved irksome. Guardians were usually drawn from the class of farmers and tradesmen whose interest was to keep as close an eye on expenditure as possible. Provided that they possessed the necessary property qualification, women were technically qualified to serve as guardians but it was forty years before the first one was elected – at Kensington, in 1875. They appeared

in numbers only after 1894, and by 1909 there were over 1200. Inevitably their attention was often directed towards 'women's work' – the care of the children and the sick – but they came to exert a great influence over the system as a whole. Working-class guardians also appeared slowly, but it was not until 1892, when the property qualification was dropped to the occupation of rented premises worth £5 annually, that workers appeared in greater numbers. It was in that year that George Lansbury and Will Crooks (both socialists, and the latter an ex-pauper) were elected in Poplar, where, under their influence, innovations in Poor Law administration soon came into being.

The key appointment which the guardians had to make was that of the master of the workhouse. In the early years of the New Poor Law the master was often seen as little more than a jailer, for the principles upon which the law was based were those of punishment rather than rehabilitation. As a consequence, suitable candidates were frequently found amongst the ranks of former policemen or non-commissioned officers in the army and navy. Typical of such men was former Staff Sergeant Colin M'Dougal, artilleryman and veteran of Waterloo, who was master of Andover workhouse at the time of the scandal there (see caption, page 25).

In 1880 Louisa Twining, a workhouse reformer, pondered 'why the appointment of master should not invariably have been given to a man of superior position...the post being one that requires great discretion and powers of government, such as we might expect to find in retired officers...' She need not have looked far for the answer, for salaries were low, duties were tiresome, there was no career structure and, until 1896, there was no right to a pension. The master was tied to the workhouse as much as the paupers themselves, if not more so. *A Guide to the... Management of Workhouses*, published in 1870, noted that the master 'should devote the whole of his time to the discharge of his duties, and he cannot be an efficient officer if he devote himself to pleasures or even to duties away from the workhouse'. The master could gain no professional qualification, for none was recognised, and better prospects of advancement were to be found by transferring to the prison service. In 1880 the master of a workhouse for between five and six hundred inmates might earn £80 a year; the governor of a prison for nine hundred prisoners could earn £600.

One qualification that a master was expected to possess was a wife, for it was standard practice (endorsed by the Commissioners in London) to appoint a married couple as master and mistress of the workhouse. For this reason it was not unknown for an unmarried workhouse schoolteacher to seek a spouse for no other reason than to climb the occupational ladder.

The role of the medical staff was crucial, especially as the sick and infirm came to comprise the majority of workhouse inmates; and in the twentieth century, doctors and nurses came to provide the link between the workhouses and the hospitals into which so many developed.

In 1842, sixteen years before the Medical Act of 1858 laid the foundations of professional status for doctors, the Poor Law Commissioners tried to insist that workhouse medical officers possessed a qualification in medicine and surgery. The work was poorly paid (at first, doctors were expected to provide drugs and medical supplies themselves) and it lacked

Women in a London workhouse receive a visit from a member of the London City Mission. Workhouses were opened up to visitors from the 1850s, and it was in 1859 that Louisa Twining, a member of the prosperous tea-importing family, took the initiative in forming the Workhouse Visiting Society. The committee included four bishops, one of whom (Robert John Eden, Bishop of Bath and Wells) had at one time been a workhouse chaplain. Louisa Twining was one of the first women to become elected to a board of guardians when that became possible in the 1880s.

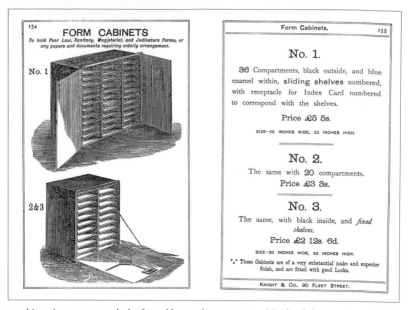

FORM CABINETS
To hold Poor Law, Sanitary, Magisterial, and Judicature Forms, or any papers and documents requiring orderly arrangement.

No. 1

2&3

Form Cabinets.

No. 1.

36 Compartments, black outside, and blue enamel within, **sliding shelves** numbered, with receptacle for Index Card numbered to correspond with the shelves.

Price £5 5s.

SIZE—29 INCHES WIDE, 22 INCHES HIGH.

No. 2.

The same with 20 compartments.

Price £3 3s.

No. 3.

The same, with black inside, and *fixed shelves.*

Price £2 12s. 6d.

SIZE—20 INCHES WIDE, 22 INCHES HIGH.

•.• These Cabinets are of a very substantial make and superior finish, and are fitted with good Locks.

KNIGHT & CO., 90 FLEET STREET.

The form cabinet is an apt symbol of workhouse bureaucracy. Much of the master's day was spent filling in forms and keeping records. In 1867 the Poor Law Board issued a General Order of Accounts which listed nearly two dozen records which had to be maintained, often on a daily basis. The Admission and Discharge Book had thirty-one columns which had to be filled in every time a pauper was admitted or let out. Most irksome was the Provisions Expenditure Book, where the master had to strike a balance between the number of paupers in the house, the weight of each type of food consumed, the amount remaining in store, and the amount of food wasted in cooking (for which the Poor Law Board laid down standard measures). At any time the guardians might demand to inspect the books, while the district auditor was expected to do so four times a year. (Illustration from the Local Government Directory, 1878.)

prestige. Nevertheless, a newly qualified doctor might take on Poor Law work to supplement his earnings from private practice, while a more experienced physician might see such work as a means of keeping out competitors.

The arrangements for the sick in the workhouse were originally rudimentary, and nursing was placed in the hands of female inmates who might be rewarded with gin for performing some of the more unpleasant tasks such as laying out the dead. Only the most basic qualifications were laid down, but Article 165 of the Consolidated Orders of 1847 did state that 'no person shall hold the office of Nurse who is not able to read directions upon medicines'. Paid nurses were at first rare, and in the 1850s there were only seventy in the whole of London, compared with five hundred pauper nurses. It was in this and the following decade that a supply of trained nurses became more readily avail-

Poor Law medical officers enjoyed a low status within the profession and were poorly remunerated; but the work might be taken on by a newly qualified doctor in order to help build up a practice in a district, or by a more experienced man anxious to keep such competition out. (Advertisement from the Northampton Mercury, 10th March 1855.)

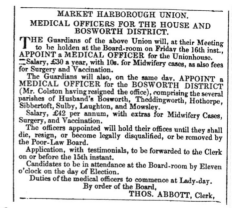

MARKET HARBOROUGH UNION.
MEDICAL OFFICERS FOR THE HOUSE AND BOSWORTH DISTRICT.

THE Guardians of the above Union will, at their Meeting to be holden at the Board-room on Friday the 16th inst., APPOINT a MEDICAL OFFICER for the Unionhouse. —Salary, £30 a year, with 10s. for Midwifery cases, as also fees for Surgery and Vaccination.

The Guardians will also, on the same day, APPOINT a MEDICAL OFFICER for the BOSWORTH DISTRICT (Mr. Colston having resigned the office), comprising the several parishes of Husband's Bosworth, Theddingworth, Hothorpe, Sibbertoft, Sulby, Laughton, and Mowsley.

Salary, £42 per annum, with extras for Midwifery Cases, Surgery, and Vaccination.

The officers appointed will hold their offices until they shall die, resign, or become legally disqualified, or be removed by the Poor-Law Board.

Application, with testimonials, to be forwarded to the Clerk on or before the 15th instant.

Candidates to be in attendance at the Board-room by Eleven o'clock on the day of Election.

Duties of the medical officers to commence at Lady-day.
By order of the Board,
THOS. ABBOTT, Clerk,

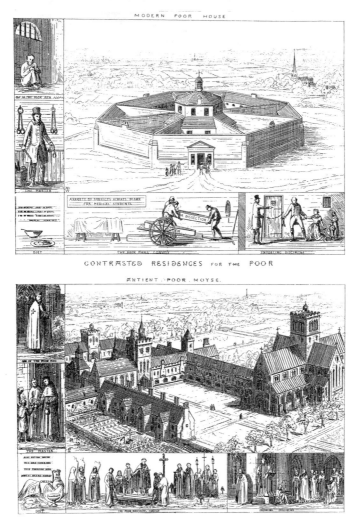

In 1841 the architect Augustus Welby Pugin published the second edition of his polemical book 'Contrasts', in which he drew 'a parallel between the noble edifices of the middle ages and corresponding buildings of the present day'. Amongst the contrasts which he drew were the residences of the poor, in which he set the workhouse alongside the medieval poor houses of the church. Not surprisingly for a work of propaganda, some of his points are unfair. Paupers did not constitute 'a variety of subjects always ready for medical students'. Medical students were admitted to workhouse infirmaries in 1867, but were banished again two years later after public fears were expressed that the poor were peculiarly vulnerable to medical experiment. No such protection was afforded to the patients of those voluntary institutions which developed into teaching hospitals.

able. It was also in the 1860s that the inadequacies of medical provision in workhouses came under close scrutiny, much of it inspired by enquiries initiated by the *Lancet*. In 1867 the Metropolitan Poor Act enabled Poor Law unions in London to act individually or in combination to establish infirmaries separate from their workhouses. In the late 1860s, and throughout subsequent decades, both in London and the provinces, much building work was carried out either to extend the infirmary provision of existing workhouses or to erect new workhouse hospitals. By 1896 nearly

Left: *Dispensaries provided a charitable means of bringing medical aid to the poor. This example, at Knaresborough in North Yorkshire, was erected in 1853 to the memory of the late vicar, the Reverend A. Cheap. In 1802, in the London area alone, fifty thousand poor patients annually are estimated to have been assisted by dispensaries.*

Below: *In 1877 a coffin for 13s 6d left little room for refinements, but at least the Andover paupers were afforded the use of a pall, denied to many. The fear of a pauper's funeral motivated thousands of working men and women in the nineteenth century to contribute weekly sums to burial clubs.*

59,000 pauper patients were being treated in workhouse sick wards or separate infirmaries.

Of lowlier status than the workhouse medical officer was the Poor Law schoolteacher. The provision of education for pauper children, like the provision of medical facilities for the destitute in general, was seen by many to conflict with the hallowed principle of less eligibility. The view prevailed, however, that children could hardly be held morally responsible for their indigence, and that education might help to break the recurring cycle of destitution. Without education, the prospects for a pauper child were dismal. A workhouse visitor in the 1880s asked a small boy idling in the yard what he hoped to do when he grew up. 'Move to the men's yard, where I can do as I like,' was the reply.

The problem was made serious by the numbers involved. Between 1834 and 1908 roughly one-third of all individuals receiving poor relief were children under sixteen; and it was not until the very end of the nineteenth century that the proportion of workhouse inmates who were children fell below a figure between one-fifth and a quarter of the whole.

Great strides were made in improving pauper education in the nineteenth cen-

ANDOVER UNION.

TENDER

For supplying the Guardians of the above Union with the Articles undermentioned.

	£	s.	d.
Coffins			
First size (including loan of pall)		13	6
Second Do			6
Third Do		4	6

accepted

To the Guardians of the Andover Union.

GENTLEMEN,

If this Tender be accepted I undertake to deliver free of expense the Articles before mentioned against which Prices are affixed (according to the Samples left herewith) at the Andover Union Workhouse for *one year* — from the *25th* day of *March* 1877 in such quantities and at such times as they shall be ordered and I undertake to execute any formal Contract to ensure the true and punctual performance of this Tender with or without two sufficient sureties as you may think advisable.

I am, Gentlemen,

Your obedient Servant,

March 23 '187*7*

Henry Wear

tury, many of them inspired by Dr James Kay (later Sir James Kay-Shuttleworth), who was an Assistant Poor Law Commissioner in East Anglia, Middlesex and Surrey. Through Kay-Shuttleworth, devel-

houses, by fostering them, or, in the case of orphans, by sending them for adoption. Even so, it was not until 1913 that the central authorities issued an order compelling the removal of children from the workhouse.

Poor Law schoolteachers, like other workhouse officials, led restricted lives. They were expected to supervise the children outside school hours and could not leave the workhouse except with the master's permission. Nor was their food any better than that of the paupers, for they received the same meals, only in larger (often inedible) portions. Such a life must have been claustrophobic but, although there were inevitable instances of cruelty towards inmates, acts of kindness by workhouse officers were not unknown, especially to those, such as the young and the old, who were thought least able to help themselves.

opments in both the curriculum and the training of teachers, which he pioneered in Poor Law schools, were extended to the mass of the country's elementary schools.

The trend was towards educating children outside the workhouse, either in Poor Law 'district schools' or in the ordinary elementary schools. There were growing moves, too, to remove children altogether from the influence of the workhouse, either by placing them in separate boarding

THE ROUTINE OF THE WORKHOUSE

A little kindness went a long way, for the routine of the workhouse was intentionally demeaning to the pauper. A man could not sacrifice himself for the sake of his family, for the ruling was that the family had to be admitted as a whole. It also had to be discharged as a group, and the head of the household had the right to discharge himself and his family at any time – the sooner, the better. Indeed, the writer Harriet Martineau envisaged the time when the master and mistress would turn the key on the front door of the now empty workhouse as all the inmates had decided to try their chances outside.

It was the porter's job to receive applicants for the workhouse, and they would be directed to the receiving ward, close to the main gate. The porter had the power to search male paupers for prohibited articles, which included alcohol, cards and dice, matches and 'letters or printed papers, as books, pamphlets, etc., being of an improper tendency'. There was an assumption that applicants for the workhouse would not be encumbered with personal possessions, and there was nowhere to keep them if they had any, other than in or under the dormitory bed. Some managed to maintain a vestige of individuality. A Devon workhouse visitor in the late 1850s described the bag which one woman had succeeded in keeping possession of: 'I have seen in it her hymn-book and spectacles, a piece of cake which I had brought her, a bit of black pudding, my letter to her, an old comb, a bit of sugar twisted up in a small piece of paper.'

Throughout the nineteenth century there was a greater proportion of old men than old women in the workhouse. Elderly women, it seemed, were less helpless than old men; being able to perform household tasks and look after children, they were more welcome in the households of the children. (Illustration from 'Living London', 1901.)

Inmates and staff of the Doncaster workhouse in South Yorkshire in the late 1890s. Typically, by this time many of the inmates had been directed to specialist institutions – to children's homes, asylums and a new hospital which Doncaster decided to build in 1900. The old workhouse was demolished in 1966. A lighter touch is given to this otherwise grim-faced group by the presence of the no doubt much loved workhouse dog, held in the arms of the porter.

The new inmates were required to wash, had their own clothes taken from them and were issued with workhouse dress. Unions were free to choose both the style of clothing and the material from which it was made. Instructions were issued in 1842 that clothes 'need not be uniform either in colour or material'; but in practice they always were, both for reasons of economy and as a badge of pauperism. However, although the law required workhouse dress to be stamped with the name of the union, the mark was supposed not to be seen when worn. Nor was penal dress allowed, except for disorderly or refractory paupers, and then only for a maximum of forty-eight hours. Such rules were often honoured in the breach. Many unions consigned unmarried mothers to 'canary wards', where they were obliged to wear a distinctive yellow uniform, or required them to wear an overdress or jacket, giving rise to the description 'jacket women'.

There were other indignities, too. Men were not permitted razors and were sometimes allowed to shave only once a week; and all inmates had their hair cut in a standard, rough and ready manner. The

These dolls, made towards the end of the nineteenth century by inmates of Thursford workhouse in Norfolk, are dressed in workhouse clothing, almost certainly from offcuts of the actual material supplied. They are now to be seen in the Norfolk Rural Life Museum, Gressenhall.

Left: *Very little workhouse clothing from the Victorian period has survived. This dress, from the Wincanton Union workhouse in Somerset, dates from the 1920s and is to be seen in the Somerset Rural Life Museum in Glastonbury.*

Below: *St Pancras workhouse in London had between fifteen hundred and two thousand inmates in 1857, of whom about two hundred were in sick wards, and one thousand were 'infirm and helpless aged persons'. To cater for the laundry work, the authorities installed a steam washing machine (with mechanical beater action) together with a 'Hydro Extractor'. The latter, revolving at nine hundred revolutions per minute, was so powerful that 'it is impossible for a strong man to wring a drop of water from the clothes, or even from blankets', once the spin-dryer had been used. (Engraving from the Illustrated London News, 3rd October 1857.)*

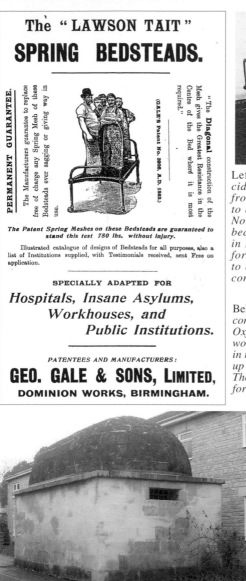

Left and above: *Woe betide any pauper who decided to put his bed to this test! (Advertisement from the Poor Law Handbook, 1903.) Worse still to apply it to the bed from Thetford workhouse, Norfolk. At Gressenhall workhouse, Norfolk, iron beds were ordered to replace older wooden ones in 1836 – double beds for women and single beds for men. Children under seven usually slept three to a bed, as did some older ones, although that contravened regulations.*

Below: *Cirencester workhouse in Gloucestershire was completed in 1837, to the design of John Plowman of Oxford. The opportunity was taken to move to the workhouse one of the town lock-ups, built in 1804-5 in nearby Gloucester Street. On its new site the lock-up became the 'refractory ward' or punishment block. The Consolidated Order of 1847 set out strict rules for the disciplining of paupers. Article 135 laid down that no pauper was to be confined between 8 p.m. and 6 a.m. without bed and suitable bedding and 'proper conveniences'. Article 136 required that no child under the age of twelve be confined in a dark room or at night.*

hair of both boys and girls was cropped, subjecting them to ridicule if they were sent to a nearby elementary school, although many unions allowed girls to grow their hair when they were ready to leave the workhouse to enter into domestic service.

The food was no less drab than the clothing. Indeed, it was the monotony of workhouse diet that was its most depressing feature. Boards of guardians were required to draw up dietaries to be approved by the central authority, and they were expected not to depart from them except on the order of the medical officer in specific cases. The staples were bread, cheese, gruel (a kind of thin oatmeal porridge), soup, potatoes and occasional meat and bacon. The quantities were rigidly set down (and had to be accounted for), and no allowance was made for appetite. Six model diets laid down by the Poor Law Board supplied between 137 and 182 ounces (3884-5160 grams) of solid food a week, which was more than

Left: Strong measures were taken against corruption in the awarding of workhouse contracts, and the Consolidated Orders of 1847 laid down that invitations for tender must be given 'in some newspaper circulating in the Union'. Local newspapers thus become a rich source for students of workhouse history. This advertisement, from Berrow's Worcester Journal, 17th September 1859, gives a good indication of the kind of food and clothing supplied to paupers at that date.

Above: Some of the most prison-like images of the workhouse are of the dining arrangements. Feeding was purely functional and left little room for dignity. These men, in a London workhouse at the start of the twentieth century, appear to be mainly the elderly. The rigidity of mealtimes could be irksome, particularly to the aged. The last meal of the day was often taken as early as 5 p.m., and the gap between then and breakfast the next morning at around 8 a.m. left the paupers without nourishment for a long period.

Below: Dietary of the workhouse at Berkhamsted in Hertfordshire, 1836. Manuscript amendments to the printed dietary make it clear that women were given a smaller allowance of bread, suet pudding and cheese than men. The Berkhamsted guardians were not alone in conducting extensive correspondence with the Poor Law authorities in London over diet and other matters. In 1843 the Poor Law Commissioners complained of the practice of handing out all the day's allowance of bread in the morning, but the guardians replied that the inmates had cupboards in the day-rooms with divisions for each person's uneaten bread.

DIETARY

of

The Workhouse of the Berkhamsted Union

	The General Dietary						Aged, Infirm, and Sick Dietary							
	Breakfast		Dinner				Supper	Breakfast		Dinner				Supper	
														Men	Men & Wom.
	Bread. oz.	Gruel. pints.	Beef. oz.	Soup. pints.	Suet Pud oz.	Potatoes lb	Cheese oz.	Broth. pints.	Bread. oz.	Gruel. pints.	Beef or Mutton	Potatoes lb	Soup. pints.	Rice Pud oz.	Cheese oz.	Broth. pints.	Women
MONDAY	14	1.5	5	-	-	1	-	1.5	10	1.5	5	1	-	-	-	1.5	Tea to be made by the Matron, and one Pint to be given to each Person twice a day, with Bread & Butter, in lieu of Gruel or Broth.
TUESDAY	14	1.5	-	1.5	-	-	2	-	10	1.5	-	-	1.5	-	2	-	
WEDNESDAY	14	1.5	5	-	-	1	-	1.5	10	1.5	5	1	-	-	-	1.5	
THURSDAY	14	1.5	-	1.5	-	-	2	-	10	1.5	-	-	1.5	-	2	-	
FRIDAY	8	1.5	-	-	14	-	2	-	10	1.5	-	-	-	10	2	-	
SATURDAY	14	1.5	5	-	-	1	-	1.5	10	1.5	5	1	-	-	-	1.5	
SUNDAY	14	1.5	-	1.5	-	-	2	-	10	1.5	-	-	1.5	-	2	-	

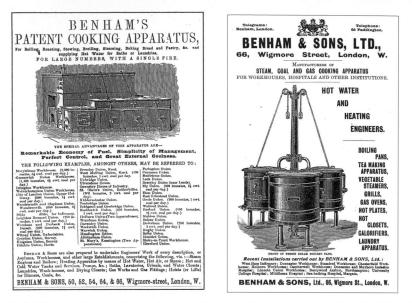

Left: The logistical problems of running large workhouses were considerable. This advertisement suggests that even with the benefit of Benham's Patent Cooking Apparatus, Marylebone workhouse, London, with two thousand inmates, was using nearly 2 tons of coal a week on cooking and water heating. (Advertisement from the Local Government Chronicle, 8th April 1876.)

Right: *In 1909 a Poor Law inspector, Herbert Preston-Thomas, recalled a workhouse visitor who had told him of the cooking arrangements in a particular institution she had been to: 'They had two coppers so set that their tops were separated only by a space of three inches. When I was there, they were boiling clothes in one and soup in the other; and there were no lids on them. When the soup boiled over into the clothes, I raised no objection, but when the clothes boiled over into the soup, I said I would not stay to dinner.' The coppers may well have been similar to these, advertised in the Poor Law Handbook of 1903 – although Benham's boilers had the merit of having lids.*

the average independent labourer was reckoned to be getting but, according to *The Times* in 1842, was around half the intake of a prisoner in jail. Workhouse food was stripped of everything that made it attractive to the poor, including in many cases the use of salt, while in some workhouses in the 1830s the inmates were even denied the use of cutlery.

Things did improve as the century progressed, as a result both of changes of attitude and greater understanding of nutrition. New General Orders, issued in 1900, allowed boards of guardians (in consultation with their medical officers) greater discretion to fix diets, which, by the turn of the century, were more generous than social investigators were finding amongst labourers either in the towns or in rural areas.

Cooking was a task usually performed by the inmates themselves, for work was an integral part of the regime for the able-bodied, while even the aged and infirm might be pressed into such tasks as teaching or looking after the children.

The actual purpose of work was never clear. The 1834 Poor Law Report was ambivalent on the subject, for the aim was to encourage paupers to leave the workhouse in order to find employment within the community. A habit of work was to be instilled, but that would not happen if work were seen to be punitive. The Report claimed that 'the association of the utility of labour to both parties, the employer as well as the employed, is one which we consider it most important to preserve and strengthen; and we deem everything mischievous which unnecessarily gives to it a repulsive aspect'. But inmates were not to be paid for their work for that would weaken the incentive to find it outside. Despite this injunction, allowances in kind (including extra food, tobacco and sometimes alcohol) continued to be made, with the inevitable consequence that there arose a hierarchy of pauper inmates in the same way that prisons had their 'trusties'.

Central administrators and local guardians often had different sets of priorities. Inmates with trade skills could save the guardians considerable sums of money by painting and decorating the workhouse, for example, although the Poor Law Inspectors frowned on a practice which could often lead to bribery. There was a limit to how many inmates could use skills in this way, and the trend in most workhouses was towards work that was tedious. Stone breaking for road repairs was common, as was oakum picking – the picking apart of old hemp ropes in order to provide the material used to caulk ships. Firewood was chopped (despite the complaints of some of the poorest independent workers that this was their living). Masters sometimes found it difficult to sell the products of such pauper labour, although at the St Marylebone workhouse in London it was duly recorded in 1892 that the 645,325 bundles of wood, 467 sacks of chips and 308 sacks of sawdust which it had sold in that year brought in to the guardians £1028 11s 4d. In the Victorian workhouse, little was left unaccounted for.

While the guardians provided work for paupers in the workhouse, they had no

Above: *The nation was shocked in 1846 when it became known that paupers in the Andover workhouse, Hampshire, were so hungry that many of them were gnawing the old bones they had been given to crush for fertiliser. This modern display in the Andover Museum faithfully reproduces the crushing boxes and the rammers that were issued to inmates in order to perform this work, a noisome task that was expressly prohibited by Article 113 of the Consolidated Orders issued in 1847.*

Below: *Inmates chopping wood in Pontefract workhouse, West Yorkshire, in the early twentieth century. Finding appropriate work for paupers to do was problematical, for it was thought undesirable to compete with independent traders, whose own livelihood might be undercut.*

MANNERS.

Discontented Pauper (on the Christmas Dinner). "Well, this is the wust Chris'mas Dinner as ever we 'ad since I 've been in the 'Ouse! I thinks as when we 'as a Dinner Party, the Master ought to ax us whether we likes it well done and whether we takes Fat, and not cut the Vittles and showl it on our Plates anyhow!"

Above: *Paupers who failed to show proper gratitude for the rare 'treats' offered them were a constant butt of middle-class humour. (Cartoon from Punch, 18th January 1879.)*

Above: *In December 1872 the artist Arthur Boyd Houghton invited a party of paupers from Islington workhouse, London, to visit his studio, where he both entertained and sketched them. The engraving which resulted was published in that year's Christmas number of the Graphic. A cripple leads a blind man who both carries another cripple and leads a second blind man. It is always difficult to know how people in the past reacted to such illustrations, but it is reasonable to assume that sentimental images of small groups of individual paupers enabled many to dismiss from their minds the problems of mass poverty.*

Left: *A New Year's Eve entertainment at the St Giles's workhouse, London, in 1881. It was noted that 550 out of the 834 inmates attended the concert. Most were aged and infirm, and for at least one (the woman in the bottom right-hand corner) enough was enough. However, 'when Mr Fred Wood gave Linley's touching ballad of "The Irish Emigrant" many of the poor old women were to be seen with tears rolling down their cheeks.' (Engraving from the Illustrated London News, 12th January 1881.)*

powers to assist an inmate to find work outside the house. A handbook for guardians published in 1871 pointed out that their 'function is to relieve destitution actually existing, and not to expend the money of the ratepayers in preventing a person from becoming destitute...they can only expend the poor-rates in supplying the destitute with actual necessaries, such as food, clothing, or lodging... Expenditure incurred for the purpose of setting a poor person up in trade, in purchasing implements or tools of trade for him....is illegal.' Guardians who so chose had ways of getting round the law. For example, one board, unable legally to contribute £5 to make up the sum of an apprenticeship premium, voted the money for 'an outfit' though, as it was pointed out, 'it was no more an outfit than a cham-

pagne dinner would have been'.

Paupers, needless to say, never were given champagne dinners, though they did have the occasional treat, especially at Christmas. It was in 1877 that George R. Sims published his ballad, popularly (but incorrectly) known as 'It was Christmas Day in the Workhouse'. Nowadays considered something of a joke, the ballad struck other chords with contemporaries, even though much of its message was inaccurate. At first the Poor Law Commissioners had forbidden any break to the harsh regime at Christmas, even if the festivities were financed by private charity, but they had to admit defeat by 1840 and seven years later authorised (but did not compel) guardians to provide Christmas extras out of the rates.

VAGRANTS

The treatment of most inmates of the workhouse became more lenient as the century progressed, although there were voices raised for a return to a harsh treatment for the 'undeserving' rather than the 'deserving' poor, a categorisation made popular by the Charity Organisation Society, founded in 1869 in order to control

indiscriminate giving and to introduce a greater element of social 'casework' into dealings with the poor.

One group whose treatment became much harsher towards the end of the century was vagrants. To the authorities 'vagrant' and 'casual' were almost synonymous, but the problem was complicated by the range of

Sir David Wilkie exhibited 'The Parish Beadle' in 1823, the year before a wide-ranging Vagrancy Act was passed. The existence of such a recent measure was undoubtedly one of the reasons why vagrants were ignored by the Poor Law Amendment Act in the following decade. Here the beadle (parish constable) escorts a number of street performers to the house of correction.

Right: *The casual ward of Marylebone workhouse, London, erected in 1867 at a cost of £1300. Two features are particularly noteworthy. The first is the bunks, which 'consist of a white deal board, supported on each side by a deal partition which rises high enough to prevent the intermingling of the breaths of the occupants of two adjoining berths, though not so high as to prevent the officials in attendance from seeing each person from any portion of the room'. The second feature is the religious texts, 'in red letters on a blue ground', that are painted on the walls and roof trusses.*

Sketches at a casual ward, from the Illustrated London News, 19th November 1887. In a clockwise direction from the bottom right-hand corner, the illustrations show: casual paupers waiting for admission; the disinfecting room; stone breaking; the bathroom; and the sleeping cells. At this time, the twenty-four casual wards of the London workhouses contained a total of between 1400 and 1500 beds.

Left and below: *Semington, the workhouse of the Melksham Union in Wiltshire, was designed in 1837 by Henry Kendall, who had previously worked for the Barrack Department of the War Office. Like many workhouses, Semington provided new wards for vagrants in the late nineteenth century. The block contained eight cells, each with space for a hammock and with a stone-breaking area. It was only when his stint of crushed stone had been passed through the grille and chute in the outer wall that the vagrant was allowed to leave. This vagrant ward was in use until 1947.*

people who fell into this category. There were those for whom 'tramping' was a way of life, and there were others who, finding themselves unemployed, were obliged to tramp in search of work. What was appropriate treatment for one group might not be so for the other.

Professional tramps had an established bush telegraph to inform each other about the severity or leniency of treatment in particular workhouses. Sometimes this extended to verse. At Whitchurch in Hampshire in 1875 fellow-tramps were offered the advice that:

The governor's name is Sutton
The pauper's diet is mutton
But you must not be a glutton
When here you lodge.
You had better go to Andover
Where you can live in clover
A far better dodge.

London was always a mecca for vagrants and, starting with the metropolis in the 1860s, draconian new regulations were introduced to solve what was seen as a mounting problem. In 1871 the Pauper Inmates Discharge and Regulation Act empowered guardians to detain casual paupers until they had performed a task of work. Here again, punishment and rehabilitation became confused, for the true work-seeker had to make an early start in order to find a job, and this the labour task prevented him from doing.

THE LAST DAYS OF THE WORKHOUSE

In 1834 the Poor Law Commission had intended out-relief for the able-bodied to be speedily abolished. This was never to be, for boards of guardians soon found loopholes in the law which enabled them to give relief outside the workhouse at a lower cost to the ratepayers. In 1846, for example, there were 1,331,000 paupers, of whom only 199,000 were to be found in the workhouse, leaving 1,132,000 on out-relief. Of these, roughly one-quarter (375,000) were able-bodied and should theoretically have been in the workhouse, but only 82,000 were to be found there. The vast majority of paupers, even the able-bodied ones, never saw the inside of a workhouse but continued to eke out a living with doles in cash or in kind from the guardians. Meanwhile, the workhouses came increasingly (though never exclusively) to house the old, the young, the sick and the mentally ill.

Towards the end of the nineteenth century social investigators such as Charles Booth in London and Seebohm Rowntree in York increased people's understanding of the complexities of poverty and pauperism. In 1905 a Royal Commission on the Poor Law was set up, but its members failed to come to any agreement. The majority issued a report which favoured keeping the existing system while subjecting it to thorough reform; the minority report favoured a scrapping of the Poor Law altogether. No immediate action was taken, but the introduction of old age pensions in 1908 and of state sickness and unemployment insurance in 1911 radically altered the situation. In 1913 workhouses became 'poor law institutions', but this was little more than a cosmetic change. It was not until 1930 that the administrative structure of the New Poor Law was finally dismantled, when the boards of guardians were dissolved and their responsibilities were handed to county and county borough councils.

Although renamed yet again (becoming 'public assistance institutions'), what most people still recognised as the workhouse lingered on until 1948. They can be found today, converted into hospitals and old people's homes, museums and luxury apartments. Age has mellowed the survivors; but they still stand as a memorial to 'Victorian values'.

From 'pauper palace' to luxury home. The workhouse at Chipping Norton in Oxfordshire was designed by George Wilkinson of Witney in about 1835. Such is the way of the world that in the mid 1990s it was converted into luxury homes.

FURTHER READING

Anstruther, Ian. *The Scandal of the Andover Workhouse*. Alan Sutton, 1984.
Bartley, George C.T. *A Handy Book for Guardians of the Poor*. Chapman & Hall, 1876.
Baxter, G.R. Wythen. *The Book of the Bastiles*. John Stephens, 1841.
Checkland, S.G. and E.O.A. (editors). *The Poor Law Report of 1834*. Penguin, 1974.
Crompton, Frank. *Workhouse Children*. Sutton, 1997.
Crowther, M.A. *The Workhouse System, 1834–1929*. Batsford, 1981.
Dickens, Anna. 'The Architect and the Workhouse', *Architectural Review*, December 1976.
Digby, Anne. *Pauper Palaces*. Routledge, 1978.
Driver, Felix. *Power and Pauperism: The Workhouse System, 1834–1884*. Cambridge University Press, 1993.
Englander, David. *Poverty and Poor Law Reform in Nineteenth Century Britain 1834–1914*. Longman, 1998.
Horn, Pamela. *Oxfordshire Village Life: The Diaries of George James Dew (1846–1928), Relieving Officer*. Beacon Publications, 1983.
Johnstone, Valery J. *Diet in Workhouses and Prisons, 1835–1895*. Garland, 1985.
Kingford, Peter, and Jones, Arthur (editors). *Down and Out in Hertfordshire*. Hertfordshire Publications, 1984.
Knott, John. *Popular Opposition to the 1834 Poor Law*. Croom Helm, 1986.
Longmate, Norman. *The Workhouse*. Pimlico, 2003.
Morrison, Kathryn. *The Workhouse*. English Heritage, 1999.
'One of Them'. *Indoor Paupers*. Chatto & Windus, 1885.
Preston-Thomas, Herbert. *The Work and Play of a Government Inspector*. William Blackwood, 1909.
Reid, Andy. *The Union Workhouse*. Phillimore, 1994.
Rogers, Joseph. *Reminiscences of a Workhouse Medical Officer*. T. Fisher Unwin, 1889.
Rose, Michael. *The English Poor Law, 1780–1930*. David & Charles, 1971.
Scott, Sir George Gilbert. *Personal and Professional Recollections*. First published 1879. Paul Watkins, 1995.
Smith, Edward. *A Guide to the Construction and Management of Workhouses*. Knight & Company, 1870.
Snell, K.D.M. *Annals of the Labouring Poor*. Cambridge University Press, 1985.
Taylor, Jeremy. *Hospital and Asylum Architecture in England 1840–1914*. Mansell, 1991.
Twining, Louisa. *Recollections of Workhouse Visiting and Management During Twenty-five Years*. Kegan Paul, 1880.
Webb, Sidney and Beatrice. *English Poor Law History*. First published 1927–9. Frank Cass, 1963.

There are many books and pamphlets on the local administration of the Poor Law, a number of which are listed by Reid. The Internet is also a valuable source of information, and sites which can be recommended include: The Union Workhouse (www.judandk.force9.co.uk/workhouse.html) and www.workhouses.org.uk, which includes the full text of the 1834 Poor Law Amendment Act.

PLACES TO VISIT

A list of workhouses which aims at comprehensive coverage will be found at the Rossbret Workhouse website (www.workhouses.co.uk), while Morrison (listed above) is a good place to start a search for surviving buildings.

Files on many workhouses, and some excellent plans and photographs, may be examined at the *National Monuments Record Centre*, Great Western Village, Kemble Drive, Swindon, Wiltshire SN2 2GZ. Telephone: 01793 414600. Website: www.english-heritage.org.uk

The principal workhouse museums are:
The Workhouse, Upton Road, Southwell, Nottinghamshire NG25 0PT. Telephone: 01636 817250. This key workhouse in Poor Law history has been restored by the National Trust and opened in March 2002. For further details contact the National Trust, East Midlands Regional Office, telephone: 01909 486411, website: www.nationaltrust.org.uk.

The Workhouse Museum of Poor Law, Sharow View, Allhallowgate, Ripon, North Yorkshire HG4 1LE Telephone: 01765 690799. Website: www.ripon.co.uk/museums

In Ireland, visit:
Donaghmore Workhouse Museum, Donaghmore, Portlaoise, County Laois. Telephone: (00353) 505 46212 or 44196. Website: www.laoistourism.ie
The Workhouse Museum, 23 Glendermott Road, Waterside, Londonderry BT48 6BG. Telephone: 028 7131 8328. Website: www.derrycity.gov.uk This is housed in a building of 1840.

Several museums housed in former workhouses contain small displays on the subject:
Nidderdale Museum, Council Offices, King Street, Pateley Bridge, North Yorkshire HG3 5LE. Telephone: 01423 711225. Website: www.nidderdalemuseum.com
Roots of Norfolk, Beech House, Gressenhall, Dereham, Norfolk NR20 4DR. Telephone: 01362 860563. Website: www.museums.norfolk.gov.uk
Thackray Museum, Beckett Street, Leeds LS9 7LN. Telephone: 0113 244 4343. Website: www.thackraymuseum.org

In addition, many museums devoted to social and local history have some material, although artefacts associated with the workhouse are rare.

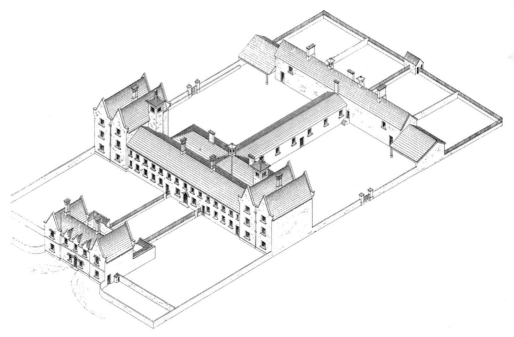

George Wilkinson designed a number of Oxfordshire workhouses before moving to Dublin in 1829 in order to become architect to the Irish Poor Law Board. In a two-year building pro-gramme, 130 workhouses were constructed, mostly following a standard plan. The workhouses tended to be larger than their English counterparts, but the standard of construction was gener-ally inferior. The day-room floors consisted of beaten earth, which Wilkinson justified not only on grounds of economy but because they were 'better adapted to the habits of the people, most of whom will be without shoes and stockings'. The bird's-eye view shown here, of a workhouse to contain between four hundred and eight hundred paupers, was published in the fifth Annual Report of the Poor Law Commissioners, 1839.